T0024648

THE
slow cooker
COOKBOOK

DEVELOPED BY

WILLIAMS SONOMA

TEST KITCHEN

Photographs Eva Kolenko

weldon**owen**

CONTENTS

Barbacoa Tacos (page 34)

Fudge Brownie Cake with
Toasted Hazelnuts (page 52)

Welcome to Slow Cooking

It's no secret why busy home cooks have been devoted to their slow cookers for years: these devices are ever-reliable for making easy and delicious dinners with minimal hands-on time. Even in the Williams Sonoma Test Kitchen, we've come to love our slow cookers for their set-it-and-forget-it nature, especially on hectic days because it frees up stovetop and oven space. With a slow cooker, you enjoy all the fabulous results from a more time-consuming, conventional recipe but with little effort in the kitchen. Just plug in the device and let the slow cooker work its magic!

Within these pages, you'll find that slow cooking takes a lot of the work out of cooking and delivers many other benefits as well. This technique boosts the flavor of dishes, reduces the amount of cooking appliances to wash, and because you don't need to keep a constant eye on cooking, frees you up to do other things while the meal nearly prepares itself.

Whether you have just a few minutes in the morning or after work to think about dinner, this book has you covered with plenty of ideas to get food on the table seamlessly. You'll find recipes developed with your busy schedule in mind, such as Pork Belly Ramen (page 18), Five-Spice Short Ribs in Lettuce Wraps (page 22), and Korean-Style Chicken with Pickled Daikon and Carrots (page 33), plus vegetarian options like Ratatouille with Balsamic & Pine Nuts (page 27) and Eggplant & Cauliflower Lasagne with Basil (page 40). Your slow cooker can even make dessert! Check out the Pear-Cornmeal Cake with Caramel Sauce (page 51) and decadent Fudge Brownie Cake with Toasted Hazelnuts (page 52). These recipes and more, including a mix of healthy and indulgent, will help you make the most of your slow cooker.

Slow-Cooking Primer

Preparing food in a slow cooker is easy, and a little extra preparation and seasoning will go a long way toward achieving delicious results. Here are a few basic steps to keep in mind. Because every model of slow cooker varies considerably, consult the manufacturer's guide before you begin.

Prepare the Ingredients To streamline the process, prep all of the ingredients in the recipe before you start cooking. That way, you'll be ready to make the dish whenever you want—now or in a few hours—and the process will be truly hands-off once the cooking starts.

Chop Smart Since denser ingredients, such as potatoes, carrots, and other root vegetables, take longer to become tender, cut them into chunks of about 1 inch or smaller. To avoid skimming extra fat from finished dishes, trim as much fat as possible off meat and poultry.

Season with Liquid Because slow cookers trap moisture with their tight-fitting lids, and therefore very little liquid evaporates during cooking, it's important to compensate with liquid flavor boosters, such as beef, chicken, fish, or vegetable broths, or soy sauce, vinegar, coconut milk, wine, and beer, instead of water.

Brown until Crisp When a recipe calls for browning ingredients before slow cooking them, take the time to do so. This is a crucial step for building flavor and adding color to the dish.

What can be cooked in a slow cooker?

- Beans and legumes
- Breads
- Curries
- Desserts, such as cakes and puddings
- Meat (bone-in and boneless)
- Pasta and noodles
- Poultry
- Risotto
- Sauces
- Seafood
- Soups
- Stews
- Stocks
- Vegetables

Moroccan-Spiced Chicken
with Chickpeas & Herbed
Lemon Couscous (page 28)

Types of Slow Cookers

There are two main types of slow cookers. The model that you own may affect the way you cook the recipes in this book. Read on to learn more about the differences.

STANDARD SLOW COOKERS

All of the recipes in this book were tested in a 7-quart standard slow cooker with a ceramic cooking insert that is not safe for stovetop use; you will need to brown, sear, and sauté ingredients in a frying pan, as instructed in the recipes, before adding them to the slow cooker. Standard slow cookers typically have a digital display with a timer and high and low heat settings; to start the device, plug it into an electrical outlet and then select the desired heat level.

ALUMINUM-INSERT SLOW COOKERS

Many newer slow-cooker models feature a cast-aluminum insert that can be used on the stovetop. If you have one of these, you can do the initial browning, searing, and sautéing directly in the insert on the stovetop, rather than in a frying pan as called for in these recipes. In most cases, you will need to brown the food in batches to avoid crowding and drain any excess fat. Do not place your slow cooker insert on the stovetop unless your model is designed for this purpose. Consult the manufacturer's guide for more information.

Slow-Cooker Safety

Because a slow cooker can reach high temperatures and release steam, treat it as you would any hot cooking device and use caution.

Place the cooker on a flat, nonporous surface, near an electrical outlet, but far from any linen, plastic, or paper material.

The Benefits of Slow Cooking

Whether you're juggling a hectic schedule and want to put wholesome, homemade meals on the table, or you just want to discover some new hearty and delicious dishes for your repertoire, a slow cooker is the answer. In addition to preparing a meal nearly hands-off, you'll enjoy other benefits as well.

- **Transform Ingredients** The slow cooker is an amazing tool for elevating humble—and economical—ingredients into something much more than the sum of their parts. Dried beans, tough cuts of meat, and starchy vegetables cooked low and slow in flavorful liquids are turned into sumptuous, fork-tender meals.

- **Free Up Time** Once the ingredients have been added to the slow cooker and the temperature and timer have been set, there's no need to stir, flip, or rotate the food, as in other conventional cooking methods. The slow cooker will free up prepping and cooking time.

- **Make It a Meal** Most of the recipes in this book combine protein, vegetables, and grains to create a full meal, so there's hardly any extra meal preparation needed. You can easily round out a slow-cooked dish by serving a simple seasonal green salad, a loaf of crusty bread, or quick-cooked sides, such as rice, quinoa, or polenta.

- **Cook Once, Eat Twice** If you own a slow cooker with a 4-quart or larger capacity, you can cook multiple servings of food, which means you'll have leftovers for more than one meal. Many of the recipes in this book, especially those with meat, freeze well, too. Avoid freezing low-fat dishes or those that include dairy.

Spicy Sesame Pork in
Cabbage Cups (page 24)

Red Lentil Curry with Green Beans

Fragrant spices are key to preparing aromatic Indian food, so double-check your spice rack to ensure items like garam masala still have potent flavor. Round out this healthy vegetarian dish with steamed long-grain rice, such as basmati.

In a large frying pan over medium-high heat, warm the oil. Add the onion and cook, stirring occasionally, until tender, about 5 minutes. Add the garlic, ginger, garam masala, turmeric, 2 teaspoons salt, and ½ teaspoon pepper and cook, stirring occasionally, until fragrant, about 1 minute. Add the chile, tomatoes with their juices, lentils, green beans, and 3 cups water and stir to combine. Transfer the mixture to a slow cooker.

Cover and cook on high according to the manufacturer's instructions until the lentils are tender, about 3 hours.

Stir the solids from the can of coconut milk into the curry until combined, then add as much liquid from the can as needed to reach the desired consistency. Remove and discard both halves of the chile.

Let the curry stand for 10 minutes to allow it to thicken slightly. Garnish with cilantro leaves and toasted coconut, if using, and serve.

Serves 4

2 tablespoons coconut oil

1 yellow onion, diced

3 cloves garlic, minced

1 tablespoon peeled and grated fresh ginger

2 teaspoons garam masala

1 teaspoon ground turmeric

Kosher salt and freshly ground pepper

1 serrano chile, seeded and halved lengthwise

1 can (15 oz) diced tomatoes with juices

1 lb red lentils, sorted and rinsed

1 lb green beans, trimmed and cut into 2-inch pieces

1 can (13.5 fl oz) coconut milk

Chopped fresh cilantro leaves, for garnish

Toasted coconut, for garnish (optional)

A single split serrano chile infuses this dish with subtle heat without overwhelming the taste. Be sure to remove both halves before serving.

If you can't find smoked ham hocks, use ¾ lb chopped smoked bacon or smoked ham. Brown the meat in a frying pan before adding it to the slow cooker to boost the flavor.

White Bean & Ham Hock Soup

Hearty and warming, this easy soup is great for a weeknight supper. Serve with simple bruschetta, which can be made quickly by toasting thick slices of country-style bread, brushing on good-quality olive oil, rubbing with a peeled garlic clove, and seasoning lightly with salt.

In a large frying pan over medium-high heat, warm the oil. Add the onion, celery, carrot, garlic, and thyme and cook, stirring occasionally, until the vegetables are slightly tender, 5–7 minutes, reducing the heat to medium if they begin to brown. Season with salt and pepper. Transfer the mixture to a slow cooker and add the ham hocks, beans, and broth.

Cover and cook on high according to the manufacturer's instructions until the ham is cooked through and the beans are just beginning to break down, about 4 hours.

Transfer the ham hocks to a cutting board. When they're cool enough to handle, remove the meat, discarding the fat, skin, and bones, and chop the meat into bite-size pieces. Return the meat to the slow cooker and stir into the beans. Cover and cook on high until the beans are creamy but still hold their shape, about 20 minutes.

Ladle the soup into bowls and garnish with the parsley and a few grindings of pepper. Serve right away.

Serves 4–6

3 tablespoons olive oil

1 yellow onion, chopped

2 ribs celery, diced

1 large carrot, diced

7 cloves garlic, thinly sliced

1 tablespoon chopped fresh thyme leaves

Kosher salt and freshly ground pepper

2 lb smoked ham hocks

3 cans (15 oz each) white beans, drained and rinsed

4 cups chicken broth

1 cup chopped fresh flat-leaf parsley

Pork Belly Ramen

This comforting noodle soup is served piping hot and flavored with healthful sea vegetables like kombu and nori. You'll find these key ingredients and others, like miso paste and mirin, at Asian markets or in the international section of many grocery stores.

In a large frying pan over medium-high heat, warm the oil. Add the lemongrass, garlic, jalapeño, and green onions and cook, stirring occasionally, until fragrant, about 3 minutes. Transfer to a slow cooker and add the broth, mirin, soy sauce, and miso. Stir to combine. Add the pork belly and kombu.

Cover and cook on high according to the manufacturer's instructions until the pork is very tender, about 4 hours.

Cook the ramen noodles according to the package instructions and divide among 4 bowls. Transfer the pork belly to a cutting board and cut into thin slices. Strain the broth, discarding the solids, and ladle into the bowls. Top with the pork belly and soft-boiled eggs. Garnish with cilantro, sesame seeds, and nori and serve right away.

Serves 4

2 tablespoons vegetable oil

1 lemongrass stalk, white part only, thinly sliced

3 cloves garlic, minced

1 jalapeño chile, seeded and thinly sliced

2 green onions, white and pale green parts, thinly sliced

4 cups chicken broth

2 tablespoons mirin

2 tablespoons soy sauce

2 tablespoons white miso

1 lb skin-on, center-cut pork belly

1 piece kombu

1 lb fresh or dried ramen noodles

4 soft-boiled eggs, peeled and halved lengthwise

Fresh cilantro sprigs, black sesame seeds, and thinly sliced nori, for garnish

For a deeper flavor, sear the pork belly in the frying pan before adding it to the slow cooker.

For more flavor, sauté the other half of the onion and add it to the slow cooker along with the chicken.

Garlicky Chicken with Parsley Salad & Broccolini

Fresh lemon and nutty Parmesan brighten these flavorful braised chicken thighs. Try serving root vegetables alongside, such as roasted sweet potatoes drizzled with balsamic vinegar or parsnips mashed with fresh herbs.

Season the chicken with salt and pepper. In a large frying pan over medium-high heat, warm the oil. Working in batches, cook the chicken until browned on both sides, about 4 minutes per side. Transfer to a slow cooker and add the wine, broth, and garlic.

Cover and cook on high according to the manufacturer's instructions until the chicken is tender, about 2 hours, adding the broccolini during the last 20 minutes of cooking.

Transfer the chicken and broccolini to a serving platter and sprinkle with the lemon zest and cheese.

In a small bowl, toss together the parsley, onion, a pinch of salt, and the lemon juice. Garnish the chicken with the parsley salad and serve right away.

Serves 4–6

3 lb skin-on, bone-in chicken thighs

Kosher salt and freshly ground pepper

2 tablespoons vegetable oil

½ cup white wine

4 cups chicken broth

12 cloves garlic, sliced

1 bunch broccolini, bottoms trimmed

Zest and juice of 1 lemon

¼ cup grated Parmesan cheese

½ cup fresh flat-leaf parsley leaves

½ red onion, thinly sliced

Five-Spice Short Ribs in Lettuce Wraps

Five-spice powder, a blend of cinnamon, anise, fennel, black pepper, and cloves, adds unique seasoning to this recipe for beef short ribs. After the lettuce wraps are stuffed with the fork-tender meat, serve them with a crunchy cucumber salad and steamed white rice alongside.

Place the shallots in a glass jar or a nonreactive bowl. In a small saucepan over high heat, combine the sugar, 1 tablespoon salt, the vinegar, and 1 cup water and bring to a simmer, stirring to dissolve the sugar and salt. Pour the liquid over the shallots and let cool to room temperature. Cover and refrigerate for at least 1 hour or up to 2 weeks.

Season the short ribs generously with salt and pepper. In a large frying pan over medium heat, warm the oil. Working in batches, cook the short ribs until browned on all sides, about 10 minutes total. Transfer to a slow cooker and add the garlic, ginger, soy sauce, fish sauce, five-spice powder, and broth.

Cover and cook on high according to the manufacturer's instructions until the meat falls apart easily when shredded with a fork, about 4 hours, flipping the ribs halfway through the cooking time.

Transfer the ribs to a bowl. When they're cool enough to handle, remove the meat, discarding the bones, and shred with 2 forks. Spoon enough of the braising sauce over the meat to just moisten.

Place about ¼ cup of the beef in the center of each lettuce leaf. Top with the pickled shallots, sprinkle with sesame seeds, and serve.

Serves 4–6

2 shallots, thinly sliced

½ cup sugar

Kosher salt and freshly ground pepper

1 cup red wine vinegar

3 lb bone-in beef short ribs

2 tablespoons vegetable oil

3 cloves garlic, minced

2-inch piece fresh ginger, peeled and minced

2 tablespoons soy sauce

2 tablespoons Asian fish sauce

1 teaspoon five-spice powder

2 cups beef broth

1 head butter lettuce, leaves separated

Sesame seeds, for garnish

Slow-Braised Beef with Tomatoes & Peppers

This beef dish, braised in a smoky tomato mixture, gets more tasty as it cooks. When you're facing a busy week, make it ahead on Sunday, then reheat the next day for an even greater depth of flavor. During the summer, try shishitos or Padróns in place of the bell peppers for a little more spice in this dish.

Season the beef generously with salt and pepper. In a large frying pan over medium-high heat, warm 2 tablespoons of the oil. Working in batches, cook the beef until browned on all sides, about 10 minutes total. Transfer to a slow cooker.

In the same pan over medium-high heat, add the onion and cook, stirring occasionally, until softened, about 3 minutes. Add the garlic and cook, stirring occasionally, until fragrant, about 1 minute. Transfer to the slow cooker and add the diced tomatoes with their juices, paprika, and a pinch of salt.

Cover and cook on high according to the manufacturer's instructions until the beef is very tender, about 4 hours.

Just before serving, in a large frying pan over high heat, warm the remaining 1 tablespoon oil. Add the bell peppers and cook, stirring frequently, until charred, about 4 minutes. Add the cherry tomatoes and cook, stirring frequently, just until they start to pop and the peppers are tender, about 2 minutes longer. Season with salt.

Serve the beef with the braising sauce and top with the bell peppers and cherry tomatoes.

Serves 4

2 lb boneless beef chuck roast, cut into 2-inch cubes

Kosher salt and freshly ground pepper

3 tablespoons olive oil

1 yellow onion, chopped

6 cloves garlic, thinly sliced

1 can (28 oz) diced tomatoes with juices

2 teaspoons smoked paprika

2 green bell peppers, seeded and cut into ½-inch slices

1 pint cherry tomatoes

Spicy Sesame Pork in Cabbage Cups

Asian ingredients like ginger, sesame oil, soy sauce, and chili garlic paste infuse the tender, slow-cooked pork tucked into these delicious cabbage cups. Sugar snap peas sautéed with fresh ginger or quick fried rice would make an excellent accompaniment.

Season the pork generously with salt and pepper. In a large frying pan over medium heat, warm the vegetable oil. Working in batches, cook the pork until browned on all sides, about 10 minutes total. Transfer to a slow cooker.

In the same pan over medium heat, add the onion and cook, stirring occasionally, until softened, about 3 minutes. Add the garlic and ginger and cook, stirring occasionally, until fragrant, about 1 minute. Transfer to the slow cooker and add ¼ cup of the soy sauce, the sesame oil, chili garlic paste, and broth. Cover and cook on high according to the manufacturer's instructions until the pork is tender and falls apart when shredded with a fork, about 4 hours.

Meanwhile, make the glaze: In a small saucepan over medium-high heat, combine the remaining ¼ cup soy sauce, the honey, vinegar, and brown sugar. Bring to a simmer and cook, stirring occasionally, until thickened, about 5 minutes. Stir in the sesame oil and chili garlic paste.

Transfer the pork to a bowl. When it's cool enough to handle, shred with 2 forks. Add the glaze and toss to coat.

Place about ¼ cup of the pork in the center of each cabbage leaf. Top with a few carrot and cucumber matchsticks, garnish with sesame seeds, and serve.

Serves 4-6

3 lb boneless pork shoulder, trimmed and cut into 2-inch pieces

Kosher salt and freshly ground pepper

2 tablespoons vegetable oil

1 yellow onion, minced

2 cloves garlic, minced

2-inch piece fresh ginger, peeled and minced

½ cup soy sauce

2 tablespoons *each* toasted sesame oil and chili garlic paste

4 cups chicken broth

¼ cup honey

2 tablespoons *each* rice vinegar, firmly packed light brown sugar, toasted sesame oil, and chili garlic paste

1 head green cabbage, leaves separated

1 carrot, peeled and cut into matchsticks

1 cucumber, peeled and cut into matchsticks

Sesame seeds, for garnish

The smaller the head of cabbage, the more tender the leaves will be. Take care when unpeeling the leaves to make sure they don't rip.

Be sure to drain the eggplant
as directed. Otherwise,
it will release a lot of liquid
as it cooks, resulting in a
watered-down ratatouille.

Ratatouille with Balsamic & Pine Nuts

The gentle heat of the slow cooker coaxes the best flavor from the eggplant, bell pepper, and other vegetables in this rustic Provençal-inspired recipe. Serve over buttered penne pasta or with crusty bread for dipping.

In a colander set in the sink or on a kitchen towel, toss the eggplant with 1 teaspoon salt. Let drain until the liquid has been released and the eggplant has darkened slightly, about 30 minutes. Pat the eggplant dry.

In a small bowl, stir together the tomato paste, oil, vinegar, garlic, thyme, 2 teaspoons salt, and a few grindings of pepper.

In a slow cooker, combine the eggplant, onion, bell peppers, zucchini, and tomatoes. Pour the tomato paste mixture over the vegetables and stir to coat. Add the capers and bay leaf and stir to combine.

Cover and cook on high according to the manufacturer's instructions until the vegetables are tender, about 4 hours. Remove and discard the bay leaf.

Just before serving, in a small frying pan over low heat, melt the butter. Add the pine nuts and toast, stirring frequently, until lightly browned and fragrant, about 3 minutes. Season with salt and sprinkle over the ratatouille. Garnish with parsley and pepper and serve right away.

Serves 4–6

1 eggplant, 1–1½ lb, cut into 1-inch cubes

Kosher salt and freshly ground pepper

5 tablespoons tomato paste

⅓ cup olive oil

6 tablespoons balsamic vinegar

4 cloves garlic, minced

2 teaspoons chopped fresh thyme leaves

1 large yellow onion, cut into 2-inch pieces

2 red bell peppers, seeded and cut into 2-inch pieces

3 zucchini, cut into 2-inch pieces

5 Roma tomatoes, seeded and cut into 2-inch pieces

⅓ cup capers, rinsed

1 bay leaf

1 tablespoon unsalted butter

½ cup pine nuts

Chopped fresh flat-leaf parsley, for garnish

Moroccan-Spiced Chicken with Chickpeas & Herbed Lemon Couscous

Hot, fluffy couscous is a traditional staple of Moroccan cuisine and takes just minutes to prepare. The couscous here, brightened by lemon and parsley, tastes even more fantastic after soaking up the delicious juices of the chicken.

Season the chicken with salt and pepper. In a small bowl, stir together the brown sugar, coriander, cumin, chili powder, garlic powder, turmeric, and ginger. Rub the spice mixture all over the chicken and refrigerate for at least 30 minutes and up to 1 hour.

In a large frying pan over medium-high heat, warm 3 tablespoons of the oil. Working in batches, cook the chicken until browned, 2–3 minutes per side. Transfer to a slow cooker.

Wipe out the frying pan with paper towels. Set the pan over medium-high heat and warm the remaining 3 tablespoons oil. Add the onions and cook, stirring occasionally, until translucent, about 5 minutes. Add the garlic and raisins and cook, stirring occasionally, for 3 minutes. Transfer the mixture to the slow cooker and add the chickpeas, broth, and wine.

Cover and cook on high according to the manufacturer's instructions until the chicken is tender, about 2 hours.

Prepare the couscous according to the package instructions and fluff with a fork. Add the butter, parsley, and lemon zest and juice and stir to combine. Season with salt and pepper.

Serve the chicken, chickpeas, and sauce over the couscous.

Serves 4

4 skin-on, bone-in whole chicken legs (about 1 lb each)

Kosher salt and freshly ground pepper

2 teaspoons firmly packed light brown sugar

1 teaspoon *each* ground coriander, ground cumin, chili powder, and garlic powder

½ teaspoon *each* ground turmeric and ground ginger

6 tablespoons olive oil

2 large yellow onions, thinly sliced

4 cloves garlic, thinly sliced

¾ cup golden raisins

1 can (15 oz) chickpeas, drained and rinsed

2½ cups chicken broth

¼ cup white wine

1½ cups couscous

2 tablespoons unsalted butter

½ cup chopped fresh flat-leaf parsley

1 teaspoon *each* grated lemon zest and fresh lemon juice

To amp up the heat,
add up to 1 teaspoon
more chili powder
to the spice rub.

Roast Beef Sandwiches with Chimichurri Mayo

To make the chimichurri, in a food processor, combine 1 cup fresh flat-leaf parsley leaves, ½ cup fresh cilantro leaves, 2 cloves minced garlic, 1 tablespoon sherry vinegar, and ¼ teaspoon red pepper flakes and pulse until chopped.

Season the beef with salt and pepper. Set aside. In a large frying pan over medium-high heat, fry the bacon until crisp, about 7 minutes. Transfer to paper towels to drain.

Pour off all but 2 tablespoons of the fat. Set the pan over high heat, add the beef, and cook until browned on all sides, about 4 minutes per side. Transfer to a slow cooker.

In the same pan over medium-high heat, add the onion, bell pepper, celery, and 1 teaspoon salt and cook, stirring occasionally, until tender, about 5 minutes. Add the garlic and cook until fragrant, about 1 minute. Add the wine and cook, stirring to scrape up the browned bits, until reduced by half, about 2 minutes. Add the broth and transfer the mixture and bacon to the slow cooker. Cover and cook on high according to the manufacturer's instructions until the meat falls apart easily when shredded with a fork, about 4 hours. Transfer to a cutting board, let rest for about 5 minutes, then shred with 2 forks.

In a large saucepan over medium heat, whisk together the butter and flour and cook, stirring constantly, until lightly toasted, about 2 minutes. Add the liquid from the slow cooker, stirring constantly, and simmer until thickened, 5-10 minutes. Stir in the meat.

In a medium bowl, whisk the chimichurri and mayonnaise until combined. Season with salt and pepper.

Spoon the beef and gravy onto the roll bottoms and top with the chimichurri mayo, cover with the roll tops and serve.

Serves 4–6

2 lb boneless beef top round or chuck roast

Kosher salt and freshly ground pepper

¼ lb bacon, diced

1 yellow onion, diced

1 green bell pepper, seeded and diced

1 rib celery, diced

3 cloves garlic, minced

½ cup red wine

3 cups beef broth

4 tablespoons unsalted butter

¼ cup all-purpose flour

1 recipe chimichurri (see note above)

½ cup mayonnaise

Kosher salt and freshly ground black pepper

4–6 French bread rolls, split

Red Wine Chicken with Shiitakes & Polenta

Earthy shiitake mushrooms combine with garlic and red wine to add layers of flavor to this chicken. The extended time in the slow cooker yields juicy, tender results with bone-in thighs (don't swap them out for a boneless alternative).

Season the chicken with salt and pepper. In a large frying pan over medium-high heat, warm the oil. Working in batches, cook the chicken, skin side down, until browned on both sides, about 3 minutes per side. Transfer to a slow cooker.

Wipe out the frying pan with paper towels. Set the pan over medium heat and melt the butter. Add the mushrooms, shallots, and garlic and cook, stirring occasionally, until the mushrooms are lightly browned and tender, about 10 minutes. Add the anchovy and capers and cook, stirring occasionally, for 1 minute. Transfer the mixture to the slow cooker and add the wine, vinegar, sage, and bay leaf.

Cover and cook on high according to the manufacturer's instructions until the chicken is tender, about 2½ hours.

In a large saucepan over medium heat, bring the milk to a simmer. When small bubbles just begin to appear, stir in the polenta. Cook, stirring constantly, until the polenta begins to set, about 2 minutes or refer to the package instructions. Stir in the cheese and cream and season with salt and pepper.

Remove and discard the bay leaf from the sauce. Serve the chicken and sauce over the polenta and garnish with parsley.

Serves 4-6

3 lb skin-on, bone-in chicken thighs

Kosher salt and freshly ground pepper

¼ cup olive oil

2 tablespoons unsalted butter

1 lb shiitake mushrooms, brushed clean, stemmed, and sliced

3 shallots, minced

5 cloves garlic, minced

1 anchovy fillet in olive oil, minced

2 tablespoons capers, rinsed

1½ cups red wine

⅓ cup balsamic vinegar

4 fresh sage leaves

1 bay leaf

3 cups whole milk

1 cup polenta or cornmeal

1 cup grated Parmesan cheese

¼ cup heavy cream

Chopped fresh flat-leaf parsley, for garnish

Gochujang is a spicy Korean condiment made from red chiles, fermented soybeans, and glutinous rice. It's available in Asian markets, many grocery stores, and online.

Korean-Style Chicken with Pickled Daikon & Carrots

This chicken has spicy but not mouth-searing heat, thanks to the thick paste called gochujang, a mainstay of Korean cooking. Don't let the remainder of the container languish—the paste works beautifully in marinades and glazes.

Season the chicken with salt and pepper. In a large frying pan over high heat, warm the canola oil. Working in batches, cook the chicken until browned on both sides, about 3 minutes per side. Transfer to a slow cooker.

In a blender, combine the orange juice, soy sauce, gochujang, brown sugar, mirin, sesame oil, yellow onion, garlic, ginger, and green onions and purée until smooth. Pour the sauce over the chicken and stir to coat.

Cover and cook on high according to the manufacturer's instructions until the chicken is tender, about 2 hours.

Meanwhile, peel the carrots and daikon into thin strips and place in a glass jar or nonreactive bowl. In a small saucepan over medium heat, combine the sugar, 1 tablespoon salt, the vinegar, and 1 cup water and bring to a simmer, stirring to dissolve the sugar and salt. Pour the liquid over the vegetables and let cool to room temperature. Cover and refrigerate for at least 1 hour or up to 2 weeks.

Serve the chicken and sauce over steamed rice and top with the pickled vegetables and green onions.

Serves 4

2 lb skinless, boneless chicken thighs

Kosher salt and freshly ground pepper

1 tablespoon canola oil

¼ cup *each* fresh orange juice and soy sauce

3 tablespoons gochujang

2 tablespoons firmly packed light brown sugar

1 tablespoon mirin

1 teaspoon toasted sesame oil

½ yellow onion, coarsely chopped

3 cloves garlic, minced

1-inch piece fresh ginger, peeled and coarsely chopped

3 green onions, white and pale green parts, thinly sliced, plus more for garnish

2 carrots

1 daikon radish

½ cup granulated sugar

1 cup rice vinegar

Steamed white rice, for serving

Barbacoa Tacos

This version of barbacoa relies on slow cooking the beef with a savory blend of spices and chiles. The resulting tender, juicy, and well-seasoned meat makes the perfect filling for tacos— top with a scattering of fresh cilantro and a squeeze of lime. Serve with pinto beans.

Season the beef with salt and pepper. In a large frying pan over medium-high heat, warm 4 tablespoons of the oil. Working in batches, cook the meat until browned on all sides, 2–3 minutes per side. Transfer to a slow cooker.

Wipe out the frying pan with paper towels. Set the pan over medium heat and warm the remaining 1 tablespoon oil. Add the white onion, garlic, cumin, and oregano and cook, stirring occasionally, until the onion is tender, about 5 minutes. Add the broth, chipotle chiles and adobo sauce, lime juice, cloves, and brown sugar and season with salt and pepper. Raise the heat to medium-high and bring the mixture to a boil. Add the bay leaves, reduce the heat to low, and simmer, stirring occasionally, for 15 minutes. Transfer the mixture to the slow cooker.

Cover and cook on high according to the manufacturer's instructions until the meat falls apart easily when shredded with a fork, about 3½ hours.

Remove and discard the bay leaves. When it's cool enough to handle, shred the beef in the slow cooker with 2 forks.

Serve the beef and sauce on warmed tortillas with the red onion, cilantro, and lime wedges.

Serves 4–6

2½ lb boneless beef chuck roast, cut into 2-inch cubes

Kosher salt and freshly ground pepper

5 tablespoons canola oil

1 white onion, diced

4 cloves garlic, minced

1 tablespoon ground cumin

1½ teaspoons chopped fresh oregano

2 cups beef broth

4 chipotle chiles in adobo sauce, chopped, plus 2 tablespoons sauce

½ cup fresh lime juice

¼ teaspoon ground cloves

2 tablespoons firmly packed light brown sugar

2 bay leaves

Warmed corn or flour tortillas, for serving

1 small red onion, diced, for serving

Fresh cilantro leaves, for serving

Lime wedges, for serving

For a richer sauce, remove
the beef from the slow cooker
before shredding. Simmer
the sauce in a large saucepan
until thickened, then stir
in the shredded beef.

Make a double batch of the gremolata and try it mixed into pasta with a little olive oil or sprinkled onto soups and stews.

Peppered Lamb Shanks with Gremolata

The best cuts of lamb for a slow cooker include lamb shanks and lamb shoulder, both of which can be tough unless cooked for a long time. In this dish, the shanks cook for eight hours at low temperature, yielding tender, melt-in-your-mouth results. Serve alongside mashed potatoes or polenta.

Season the lamb generously with salt, then press each shank into the peppercorns to coat all sides.

In a large frying pan over high heat, warm 1 tablespoon of the oil. Working in batches, cook the lamb until browned on all sides, about 8 minutes total. Transfer to a slow cooker, placing the shanks in a single layer as much as possible.

In the same pan over medium heat, warm the remaining 1 tablespoon oil. Add the shallots and 1 teaspoon salt and cook, stirring occasionally, until the shallots are tender, about 5 minutes. Add half of the garlic, the rosemary, and tomato paste and cook, stirring occasionally, until fragrant, about 1 minute. Add the wine and bring to a boil, then reduce the heat to medium and simmer. Cook until the wine is reduced to about ½ cup, about 10 minutes. Stir in the broth and transfer the mixture to the slow cooker. Cover and cook on low according to the manufacturer's instructions until tender, about 8 hours.

Transfer the lamb shanks to a platter and cover loosely with aluminum foil. Skim off any fat from the surface of the sauce. Using a blender, purée the sauce until smooth. Transfer the sauce to a saucepan over high heat and bring to a boil. Cook until the sauce thickens, about 15 minutes. Remove from the heat and stir in the butter.

In a small bowl, stir together the lemon zest, parsley, and the remaining garlic. Top the lamb shanks with some sauce and gremolata. Serve with the remaining sauce and gremolata.

Serves 4

4 lamb shanks
(about 1 lb each)

Kosher salt

1 tablespoon coarsely
ground peppercorns

2 tablespoons olive oil

4 large shallots, minced

5 cloves garlic, minced

1 tablespoon minced
fresh rosemary

1 teaspoon tomato paste

2 cups red wine

2 cups beef broth

3 tablespoons unsalted
butter

Zest of 1 lemon

¼ cup minced fresh
flat-leaf parsley

Baked Pasta with Pumpkin, Kale & Gruyère

Delicious and substantial, this unfussy dish is a versatile option for weeknight suppers. Depending on what ingredients you have on hand, you could substitute spinach or chard for the kale or add a meaty touch with diced ham.

In a slow cooker, stir together the whole milk, evaporated milk, pumpkin purée, mustard, nutmeg, and ½ teaspoon salt. Add the pasta, cheese, and kale and stir to coat. Cover and cook on high according to the manufacturer's instructions for 2½ hours.

In a large frying pan over medium heat, melt the butter. Add the panko and stir to coat. Cook, stirring frequently, until the bread crumbs are lightly golden brown, about 4 minutes. Stir in the sage and cook until the bread crumbs are deep golden brown, about 2 minutes longer. Remove from the heat.

Sprinkle the bread crumbs on the pasta and finish cooking uncovered, about 30 minutes longer.

Serves 6

2 cups whole milk

2 cans (12 fl oz each) evaporated milk

1 can (15 oz) pumpkin purée

1 teaspoon Dijon mustard

½ teaspoon ground nutmeg

Kosher salt

1 lb dried pasta shells

½ lb Gruyère cheese, grated (3 cups)

2 cups coarsely chopped kale

4 tablespoons unsalted butter

1 cup panko bread crumbs

1 tablespoon finely chopped fresh sage leaves

Artichoke & Spinach Risotto with Goat Cheese

The constant stirring required by most risotto recipes is a thing of the past when you prepare this Italian dish in a slow cooker. This creamy vegetarian version, dotted with bright green spinach and fresh goat cheese, is a sure hit.

In a large frying pan over medium heat, melt the butter. Add the onion and cook, stirring occasionally, until softened, about 3 minutes. Add the garlic and cook, stirring occasionally, until fragrant, about 1 minute. Add the wine and cook, stirring to scrape up the browned bits, until thickened, about 3 minutes. Add the rice and cook, stirring frequently, until lightly toasted, about 3 minutes. Transfer to a slow cooker and add 1 tablespoon salt, the broth, and artichoke hearts. Stir to combine.

Cover and cook on low according to the manufacturer's instructions until the rice is tender, 2–3 hours.

Stir in the spinach and goat cheese. Cover and cook on low until the spinach is wilted, about 5 minutes. Season with salt and pepper and serve right away.

Serves 4

4 tablespoons unsalted butter

1 yellow onion, chopped

2 cloves garlic, minced

½ cup white wine

2 cups Arborio rice

Kosher salt and freshly ground pepper

4 cups chicken or vegetable broth

2 cans (8 oz each) artichoke hearts, drained

2 cups baby spinach leaves

¼ lb crumbled goat cheese

Eggplant & Cauliflower Lasagne with Basil

The slow cooker is a foolproof way to make lasagne because it stays moist and cooks evenly, which can be challenges when its prepared in the oven. If you have some meat eaters at the table, consider serving a side dish of grilled Italian sausages and peppers.

Lightly oil the bottom and sides of a slow cooker.

In a large frying pan over medium heat, warm the oil. Add the onion and cook, stirring occasionally, until softened, about 3 minutes. Add the garlic and cook, stirring occasionally, until fragrant, about 1 minute. Add the eggplant and cauliflower and cook, stirring occasionally, until the vegetables are slightly softened, about 10 minutes. Season with salt and pepper and remove from the heat.

In a bowl, stir together the ricotta and milk until smooth. Stir in the chopped basil and season with salt and pepper.

Spread half of the tomato sauce on the bottom of the slow cooker. Cover with a single layer of lasagne noodles. Spread one-third of the ricotta mixture on top, then top with one-third of the vegetable mixture. Sprinkle with one-fourth each of the mozzarella and Parmesan. Repeat the layering of noodles, ricotta, vegetables, mozzarella, and Parmesan two more times. Cover with the remaining noodles, then top with the remaining tomato sauce, mozzarella, and Parmesan.

Cover and cook on low according to the manufacturer's instructions until the vegetables are tender, about 3 hours.

Let the lasagne rest for 15 minutes before serving. Garnish with basil leaves and serve warm.

Serves 8

3 tablespoons olive oil, plus more for greasing

1 yellow onion, diced

3 cloves garlic, minced

1 eggplant, thinly sliced

1 cauliflower, cut into florets

Kosher salt and freshly ground pepper

18 oz ricotta cheese

¼ cup whole milk

2 tablespoons finely chopped fresh basil, plus whole leaves, for garnish

3 cups store-bought or homemade tomato sauce

1 lb lasagne noodles

1 lb mozzarella cheese, shredded (6 cups)

6 oz Parmesan cheese, grated

Use classic ruffle-edged lasagne noodles for this recipe; no-boil noodles become too soft during cooking, so the lasagne will lose its structure.

If you can't find harissa,
any red chili-based hot
sauce will work just fine;
the thicker the better.
Leftover stew freezes
well for up to 3 months.

Harissa Beef Stew with Mint-Orange Yogurt Sauce

Harissa, an aromatic chile paste widely used in North African and Middle Eastern cooking, adds undeniable heat to any dish. Here, that spicy element is balanced by a refreshing yogurt sauce spiked with bright citrus and cool mint.

Season the beef with salt and black pepper. In a large frying pan over medium-high heat, warm the oil. Working in batches, cook the beef until browned on all sides, 2–3 minutes per side. Transfer to a slow cooker.

In a small bowl, stir together the paprika, coriander, turmeric, cumin, ginger, and cayenne. Sprinkle the spice mixture over the beef and stir to coat. Add the onion, carrots, potatoes, and garlic to the slow cooker. In a large bowl, whisk together the broth and harissa. Pour over the beef and vegetables.

Cover and cook on high according to the manufacturer's instructions until the meat is tender, about 4 hours.

In a small bowl, stir together the yogurt, mint, and orange zest.

Ladle the beef stew into bowls and top with the yogurt sauce and more mint, orange zest, and harissa. Serve right away.

Serves 4–6

3 lb boneless beef chuck roast, cut into 2-inch cubes

Kosher salt and freshly ground black pepper

¼ cup olive oil

1 teaspoon sweet paprika

½ teaspoon *each* ground coriander, ground turmeric, ground cumin, and ground ginger

¼ teaspoon cayenne pepper

1 yellow onion, diced

2 large carrots, peeled and cut into 1-inch pieces

1 lb Yukon gold potatoes, peeled and cut into 1-inch pieces

3 cloves garlic, sliced

4 cups beef broth

¼ cup harissa, plus more for serving

1 cup plain whole-milk Greek yogurt

1 tablespoon chopped fresh mint, plus more for garnish

3 teaspoons grated orange zest, plus more for garnish

Barbecue Pulled Pork with Corn Bread Top

Rich corn bread topping made with corn kernels is layered over luscious pulled pork in this meaty dish. Serve with a creamy potato salad, crunchy apple-and-carrot slaw, or crisp green salad with a simple shallot vinaigrette.

In a saucepan over medium-high heat, combine the ketchup, 1½ cups water, the vinegar, brown sugar, Worcestershire sauce, chipotle powder, onion powder, dry mustard, and garlic powder and bring to a boil. Reduce the heat to low and simmer, stirring frequently, until slightly thickened and darkened, 20–25 minutes. Set the barbecue sauce aside.

Season the pork with salt and pepper. In a large frying pan over medium heat, warm 4 tablespoons of the oil. Working in batches, cook the pork until browned on all sides, about 10 minutes total per batch. Transfer to a slow cooker.

Set the pan over medium heat and warm the remaining 1 tablespoon oil. Add the onion and cook, stirring occasionally, until tender, 3–5 minutes. Transfer to the slow cooker. Pour over the barbecue sauce and stir to coat. Cover and cook on high according to the manufacturer's instructions until the pork is tender, about 3 hours. When it's cool enough to handle, shred the pork in the slow cooker with 2 forks.

In a large bowl, whisk together the flour, cornmeal, baking powder, and 1 teaspoon salt. In a small frying pan over medium-low heat, brown the butter. Remove from the heat and stir in the corn; let cool slightly. Make a well in the center of the flour mixture. Add the corn mixture, brown sugar, eggs, and milk and stir until well combined. Spoon the batter evenly over the pork. To prevent condensation dripping on the corn bread, line the underside of the lid with a paper towel. Cover and cook on high until a toothpick inserted in the corn bread center comes out clean, about 1 hour. Serve right away.

Serves 6–8

2 cups ketchup

½ cup cider vinegar

¼ cup plus 3 tablespoons firmly packed light brown sugar

2 teaspoons Worcestershire sauce

1½ teaspoons chipotle chile powder

1 teaspoon *each* onion powder and dry mustard

½ teaspoon garlic powder

3 lb pork shoulder, trimmed and cut into 2-inch pieces

Kosher salt and freshly ground pepper

5 tablespoons olive oil

1 large yellow onion, diced

1 cup *each* all-purpose flour and yellow cornmeal

2 teaspoons baking powder

5 tablespoons unsalted butter

¾ cup fresh or thawed frozen corn kernels

2 tablespoons firmly packed light brown sugar

2 large eggs, lightly beaten

½ cup whole milk

Mole-Braised Pork Shoulder

Traditional Mexican mole uses a complex blend of spices and chocolate to achieve its rich, complex, and satisfying flavor. In this version, a welcome touch of smoky heat comes from chipotle chile in adobo, a versatile pantry staple.

Season the pork with salt and pepper. In a large frying pan over medium heat, warm the oil. Add the pork and cook until browned on all sides, about 10 minutes total. Transfer to a slow cooker.

In the same pan over medium heat, add the onion and cook, stirring occasionally, until softened, about 3 minutes. Add the garlic and cook, stirring occasionally, until fragrant, about 1 minute. Transfer to the slow cooker and add 2 cups water, the almonds, tomato paste, chipotle chile, cumin, paprika, cloves, chili powder, cinnamon stick, and chocolate.

Cover and cook on high according to the manufacturer's instructions until the pork falls apart easily when shredded with a fork, about 4 hours.

Transfer the pork to a large bowl. When it's cool enough to handle, shred with 2 forks. Remove and discard the cinnamon stick. Transfer 3 cups of the sauce to a saucepan set over medium heat and bring to a simmer. Cook until thickened, about 10 minutes. Season with salt and pepper.

Transfer the pork to a serving platter and pour the sauce over the top. Serve with warmed tortillas, cilantro, and sour cream.

Serves 4-6

3 lb pork shoulder, trimmed

Kosher salt and freshly ground pepper

2 tablespoons vegetable oil

1 yellow onion, thinly sliced

3 cloves garlic, thinly sliced

¼ cup toasted almonds, chopped

3 tablespoons tomato paste

1 chipotle chile in adobo sauce, chopped

1 tablespoon ground cumin

1 tablespoon smoked paprika

1 teaspoon ground cloves

1 teaspoon chili powder

1 cinnamon stick

2 oz semisweet chocolate, chopped

Warmed corn or flour tortillas, for serving

Chopped fresh cilantro and sour cream, for serving

Brown Sugar Pulled Chicken Sandwiches with Green & Red Cabbage Slaw

Flavored with tangy vinegar and sweet brown sugar, this chicken is a delicious, leaner alternative to traditional pulled pork. Layering the tender meat with crunchy slaw on a pretzel bun makes a sandwich hearty enough for dinner.

Season the chicken with salt and black pepper. In a large frying pan over high heat, warm the oil. Working in batches, cook the chicken until browned on both sides, about 3 minutes per side. Transfer to a slow cooker.

In a small bowl, whisk together the brown sugar, cider vinegar, tomato paste, 1 tablespoon Dijon mustard, the Worcestershire sauce, paprika, garlic powder, cayenne, and dry mustard. Season with salt and black pepper, then whisk in the broth. Pour over the chicken. Cover and cook on high according to the manufacturer's instructions until the chicken falls apart when shredded with a fork, about 2 hours.

Transfer the chicken to a cutting board. When it's cool enough to handle, shred with 2 forks.

Transfer the sauce to a large saucepan, over medium-high heat, and bring to a simmer. In a small bowl, whisk together the cornstarch and 1 tablespoon cold water and stir into the sauce. Simmer until the sauce thickens, about 3 minutes. Add the chicken and stir to coat.

Meanwhile, in a large bowl, combine the cabbages and onion. In a small bowl, whisk together the mayonnaise, the remaining 2 teaspoons Dijon mustard, and the white wine vinegar and pour over the slaw. Sprinkle with poppy seeds, season with salt and black pepper and toss to combine.

Spoon the chicken and sauce on the bun bottoms, top with the slaw, cover with the bun tops, and serve.

Serves 4-6

3 lb skinless, boneless chicken thighs

Kosher salt and freshly ground black pepper

1 tablespoon olive oil

½ cup firmly packed light brown sugar

2 tablespoons *each* cider vinegar and tomato paste

1 tablespoon plus 2 teaspoons Dijon mustard

1 tablespoon Worcestershire sauce

1 teaspoon *each* smoked paprika and garlic powder

¼ teaspoon *each* cayenne pepper and dry mustard

½ cup chicken broth

1 tablespoon cornstarch

2 cups *each* thinly sliced napa and red cabbage

¼ cup *each* minced red onion and mayonnaise

2 teaspoons white wine vinegar

1 tablespoon poppy seeds

6-8 pretzel buns, split

A slurry, which combines equal parts cornstarch and cold water or broth, is used to thicken sauces and soups. For a thicker sauce, add more slurry.

We recommend using frozen blueberries instead of fresh ones for this dessert as frozen berries provide a smoother texture.

Blueberry-Oat Crisp

This crowd-pleasing dessert with a crunchy golden topping and sweet blueberry filling can be made all year long since it's prepared with frozen fruit. If you prefer the look and flavor of mixed berries, replace half of the blueberries with frozen raspberries.

In a slow cooker, combine the blueberries, lemon juice, ⅓ cup of the sugar, and ¼ cup of the flour and stir to coat the berries.

In a bowl, whisk together the remaining ⅓ cup sugar and ¾ cup flour, the oats, cinnamon, and ¼ teaspoon salt. Using your fingers, mix in the butter until it is mostly distributed and crumbly. Sprinkle the flour mixture evenly over the blueberry mixture.

Cover and cook on high according to the manufacturer's instructions until the topping is crisp and golden, about 3½ hours. If it is not, continue to cook for up to 1 hour longer.

Serve the crisp warm with whipped cream.

Serves 4

1 package (15 oz) frozen blueberries

1 tablespoon fresh lemon juice

⅔ cup sugar

1 cup all-purpose flour

¾ cup rolled oats

1½ teaspoons ground cinnamon

Kosher salt

½ cup cold unsalted butter, cut into ½-inch cubes

Whipped cream, for serving

Tiramisu Bread Pudding

All the decadent flavors of Italian tiramisu are packed into this delicious bread pudding. Don't skimp on the amount of time the bread soaks in the creamy mixture; it must be fully saturated to make a custard-like quality when cooked.

In a large bowl, whisk together the milk, 1⅓ cups cream, 3 tablespoons espresso powder, the eggs, sugars, ½ teaspoon salt, cocoa powder, and vanilla. Add the bread, submerging it completely in the milk mixture, and let soak for 15 minutes. Transfer to a slow cooker.

Cover and cook on low according to the manufacturer's instructions for 3 hours.

Meanwhile, in a small bowl, whisk together the remaining 2 tablespoons cream, confectioners' sugar, and the remaining ½ teaspoon espresso powder. After the pudding has cooked for 3 hours, pour the glaze evenly on top. Cover and cook on high until the glaze has melted and the bread pudding is completely cooked through, about 30 minutes longer.

Just before serving, in a medium bowl, stir together the mascarpone, 5 tablespoons cream, the sugar, and vanilla. Top the bread pudding with the mascarpone mixture, dust with cocoa powder, and serve.

Serves 6–8

1⅓ cups whole milk

1⅓ cups heavy cream, plus 2 tablespoons

3 tablespoons instant espresso powder, plus ½ teaspoon

4 large eggs, lightly beaten

½ cup granulated sugar

½ cup firmly packed light brown sugar

Kosher salt

3 tablespoons unsweetened cocoa powder

1 tablespoon pure vanilla extract

8 cups cubed French bread (1-inch cubes)

5 tablespoons *each* heavy cream and confectioners' sugar

1 cup mascarpone cheese

3 tablespoons granulated sugar

½ teaspoon pure vanilla extract

Unsweetened cocoa powder, for dusting

Pear-Cornmeal Cake with Caramel Sauce

A rich caramel sauce makes this easy cake featuring sweet pear, fragrant cinnamon, and crunchy pecans irresistible. Serve this comforting dessert warm with scoops of vanilla ice cream.

Lightly butter the bottom and sides of a slow cooker.

In a large bowl, whisk together the flour, cornmeal, granulated sugar, ½ cup of the brown sugar, baking powder, cinnamon, ginger, and ¼ teaspoon salt. Stir in the milk and 1 teaspoon vanilla until the batter is smooth, then stir in the pears and ½ cup of the pecans. Transfer the batter to the slow cooker and spread evenly.

Cover and cook on high according to the manufacturer's instructions until the center of the cake is dry to the touch, about 3 hours. To prevent condensation dripping on the cake, line the underside of the lid with a paper towel during the last hour of cooking.

Just before serving, make the caramel sauce: In a saucepan over medium-low heat, combine the remaining 1 cup brown sugar, cream, and butter. Cook until the butter is melted, then stir to combine. Raise the heat to medium and cook, stirring occasionally, until the sauce is thick enough to coat the back of a spoon, about 5 minutes. Remove from the heat and stir in the remaining 1 tablespoon vanilla.

Pour the caramel sauce over the cake, sprinkle with the remaining ½ cup pecans, and serve warm.

Serves 6-8

4 tablespoons unsalted butter, plus more for greasing

2 cups all-purpose flour

1 cup yellow cornmeal

½ cup granulated sugar

½ cup firmly packed light brown sugar, plus 1 cup

1 tablespoon baking powder

1 teaspoon ground cinnamon

½ teaspoon ground ginger

Kosher salt

1¾ cups whole milk

1 teaspoon pure vanilla extract, plus 1 tablespoon

4 pears (about 1 lb total weight), peeled and thinly sliced

1 cup chopped pecans

½ cup heavy cream

Fudge Brownie Cake with Toasted Hazelnuts

Toasting hazelnuts intensifies their flavor and lends them a crisp texture. Here, they add a decadent final touch to this luscious dessert. Toast the nuts in a dry frying pan over medium heat, stirring frequently, until golden.

Lightly butter the bottom and sides of a slow cooker.

In the slow cooker, whisk together the flour, sugar, cocoa powder, baking powder, and 1 teaspoon salt. In a small bowl, dissolve the espresso powder in the hot water and set aside.

In a medium bowl, stir together the melted butter, milk, sour cream, eggs, and vanilla. Add the espresso mixture and stir to combine. Slowly add the butter mixture to the flour mixture and stir to combine; do not overmix. Fold in the chocolate chips.

Cover and cook on high according to the manufacturer's instructions until the edges are crisp and the center is fudgy, about 3 hours. To prevent condensation dripping on the cake, line the underside of the lid with a paper towel during the last hour of cooking.

Using a serving spoon, transfer the brownie cake to individual bowls and let cool slightly. Serve warm, topped with vanilla ice cream and sprinkled with the hazelnuts.

Serves 6–8

5 tablespoons unsalted butter, melted and cooled, plus more for greasing

2 cups all-purpose flour

2 cups sugar

¼ cup plus 2 tablespoons unsweetened cocoa powder

2 teaspoons baking powder

Kosher salt

1 tablespoon instant espresso powder

2 tablespoons hot water

¾ cup whole milk

½ cup sour cream

2 large eggs, lightly beaten

1 teaspoon pure vanilla extract

¾ lb semisweet chocolate chips

Vanilla ice cream, for serving

1 cup hazelnuts, toasted and chopped, for serving

For serving, try other combinations of frozen treats and crunchy nuts, such as caramel gelato with toasted almonds or strawberry ice cream with crushed pistachios.

Index

The Slow Cooker Cookbook

Conceived and produced by Weldon Owen, Inc.
in collaboration with Williams Sonoma, Inc.
3250 Van Ness Avenue, San Francisco, CA 94109

A WELDON OWEN PRODUCTION
1045 Sansome Street, Suite 100
San Francisco, CA 94111
www.weldonowen.com

WELDON OWEN, INC.
President & Publisher Roger Shaw
SVP, Sales & Marketing Amy Kaneko
Finance & Operations Director Philip Paulick

Associate Publisher Amy Marr
Associate Editor Emma Rudolph

Creative Director Kelly Booth
Art Director Marisa Kwek
Senior Production Designer Rachel Lopez Metzger
Production Designer Howie Severson

Production Director Chris Hemesath
Associate Production Director Michelle Duggan
Imaging Manager Don Hill

Photographer Eva Kolenko
Food Stylist Lillian Kang
Prop Stylist Alessandra Mortola

Copyright © 2016 Weldon Owen, Inc.
and Williams Sonoma, Inc.
All rights reserved, including the right of reproduction
in whole or in part in any form.

Printed in China
First printed in 2017
10 9 8 7 6 5 4 3 2

Library of Congress Cataloging-in-Publication
data is available.

ISBN: 978-1-68188-218-5

Weldon Owen is a division of Bonnier Publishing USA
www.bonnierpublishingusa.com

ACKNOWLEDGMENTS

Weldon Owen wishes to thank the following people for their generous support
in producing this book: Kris Balloun, Lesley Bruynesteyn, Kate Chynoweth,
Gloria Geller, Alexis Mersel, Elizabeth Parson, Nik Sharma,
Sharon Silva, Rosanna van Straten, and Xi Zhu.